I0490910

REAL ESTATE GIANTS

ALL YOU NEED TO KNOW

By

JAMES T FISK

Copyright .© by James T. Fisk 2023. All right reserved.

Before this document is duplicated or reproduced in any manner, the publisher's consent must be gained. Therefore, the contents within can neither be stored electronically, transferred, nor kept jn a database. Neither in part nor full can the document be copied, scanned, faxed or retained without approval from the publisher or creator

Introduction

Each and every individual who has a go at something new begins as a tenderfoot. That is reality. Despite the fact that I have purchased, sold, possessed,what's more, dealt with an enormous land portfolio and presently help others get everything rolling in the land, I started the race at the beginning line like every other person. To demonstrate it here is my Genuine Bequest Tenderfoot history.

To start with, let me start by letting you know that there is nothing mind-blowing about me or my capacity to make progress. In school, I endeavored to get normal grades. I went to school, however, I didn't succeed there immediately. I fizzled, as a matter of fact,

a bookkeeping class-andI was a bookkeeping major! I moved to an alternate college and in the end graduated with a degree in broad daylight bookkeeping and money. After school, I began working for a public bookkeeping firm, one | had interned for while still in school. I proved unable to sit tight for the day when I'd accept my most memorable full-time compensation offer. I was prepared to be paid boatloads of money at last. In any case, to spare the nitty-gritty details, when that hotly anticipated offer came, I was really disheartened.

The dollar sum stunned me. It was so low! At the point when I

at long last grasped all that I had been working for, I

have left inclination not exactly fulfilled. I chatted with

another worker and shared my mistake. She was the most youthful accomplice at the firm, a fruitful lady I respected monstrously. Through her, I discovered that even the accomplices (the big enchiladas at the firm) didn't make "fantastic cash" even following quite a while of difficult work and extended periods of time. That second was one I will always

remember. I would have rather not been her. I didn't need what she had. I needed more.

Be that as it may, I didn't have any idea what else to do. While I didn't adore my profession, I actually had the thought in my mind that a task was a work. A task was a need. So I bit the bullet and dissatisfaction, and I remained. I worked at the firm for around a half year. During that time, I began reading up for my CPA test and took the first of the four required tests. I fizzled. I was so humiliated.

Perhaps I wasn't great at being a bookkeeper; perhaps I had squandered my certification; perhaps I would be bankrupt until the end of time. When charge season came around, every day turned out to be more difficult than the last. I would have rather not gone to work. Despite the fact that I'd endeavored to show up at this objective, I needed out.

The possibility of expenditure the remainder of my life like this killed

me. I needed to head off to someplace else. To accomplish something different. I chatted with my better half, and his unpolished response was

"Indeed, if you need to go an extra mile on the ranch, I figure you should stop." I put in my two weeks notification, and after seven days figured out I was pregnant. It appeared to be intended to be.

Following six weeks as a pregnant stay-at-home destined to-be

mother, I was moved by a family companion to help him put together his business. It was a transient appointment where I

could work from my comfort and generate my own hours. I wasn't

great at sitting idle, so this appeared to be a decent

arrangement. The "coordinate" some portion of the gig turned out to be

dealing with a forty-unit high rise. Without even understanding what a property director was, out of nowhere, Iwas one. I was shown my arrangement a little office with no Windows or AC, a cabinet brimming with keys, and a crate loaded with leases. In that little office, I began a property

the executives' organization and developed the mental fortitude to begin

contributing myself (after I had my moment of clarity).

This moment of realization came from working for this financial backer.

In addition to the fact that I saw firsthand the properties and organizations

he possessed, however, he likewise let me help and advance along the

way. At the point when I initially began, he was getting another business,

bought in real money. I was unable to appreciate how somebody

could simply have that much money laying around, however, I learned

rapidly that it wasn't simply sitting in heaps around his home.

All things considered, he told me the best way to assist him with renegotiating one of his high rises that had valued in esteem.

He took another home loan on the property and utilized the cash he'd acquired in new value to buy the business.

The high rise's rental pay was paying the

home loan, and he was utilizing the assets from the renegotiate

to purchase this new business that would produce more

pay for him. My brain went at an impressive rate. It would have taken me years-perhaps many years to procure and save

enough money to purchase a business, and here this financial backer was

utilizing cash into more cash, into more cash

once more! At the end table, he let me work out the checks. It
was more cash than I at any point figured I would compose a check
for. The effect this second had on me can't be
downplayed l acknowledged both that | needed to be the one
marking those checks one day and that it could really
be workable for me. Over the course of the following couple of months, I conversed with his child about putting resources into land with me. Within a
year, we pulled the trigger and purchased our most memorable duplex. That was only the start, however, I had a challenging situation to deal with.
After four years, in 2018, I was thirty, wedded with three kids, and residing in the fantasy house my better half and I assembled furthermore, I was $169,000 underwater. This obligation was from a line of
credit, ranch hardware, understudy loans, and our vehicles, furthermore, the regularly scheduled installments added up to $3,712. I wish this was an emotional poverty to newfound wealth story for your diversion, yet, it's not. Every month, we covered our bills. We didn't really
battle, however, we didn't flourish. I was making around $35,000
a year at my W-2 and my better half's homestead pay found the middle value of around $60,000 every year. We had under $5,000 in
reserve funds. Everything appeared to be typical until | tracked down Dave Ramsey and his at times disruptive obligation-free arrangement. He enlivened me to get out of private obligation. I began taking the entirety of my

income from the little rental portfolio I'd developed and paying off
our own obligation. We did it in over two years. I
truly couldn't say whether we might have done it without my
rental portfolio. There are such countless feelings on whether
you ought to escape obligation prior to effective money management or then again assume you ought to
simply make a plunge. I won't offer you a solitary response on
that-l accept you ought to pick what you want. For
us, settling obligations and contributing at the same time was
the most ideal choice.
The solution for me is to begin flourishing throughout everyday life, as you can likely supposition by the title of this book, was land.
Since that first property buy in 2014, finding
BiggerPockets in 2017 (when I significantly increased my portfolio thanks
to the assets I tracked down there), and escaping individual obligation, I have totally changed my life. I went from
steadiness to creating financial well-being, and I saw the absolute most
development in my self-improvement. Having something you are energetic and amped up for can be
groundbreaking. At first, I needed to purchase venture property on the grounds that needed to be affluent. I needed the
additional pay. I needed to get free from our obligation and

to be work-discretionary. In any case, when I was in money management, I understood the amount I needed to be unconstrained. I needed to be
secure and have time opportunity. Land got me there.
When I characterized my "why" (living unexpectedly and not
being bound to a task or set pay), I turned out to be much more
spurred and centered.
In under 10 years, have made two properties
for the executives' organizations, opened a wine and alcohol store,
fabricated an arrangement of the north of thirty units in private and
business land, and left on numerous other
irregular undertakings. This will presumably be the
hardest passage I need to write in the book, since it's
where I'm expected to feature my achievements so
you know I'm genuine and ought to pay attention to me. Actually, I've
had similar however many disappointments as I have had triumphs.
Everyone makes mistakes, thus a lot of life is an investigation. I
committed my reasonable portion of errors en route. In this book, need to impart to you both my triumphs and
entanglements; outfitted with the two pieces, you can be more
fruitful and arrive at your objectives much more rapidly than I
did (with less experimentation than it took me). The "why" I
began with such a long time back has moved and turned.

In any case, the magnificence of land is that a vehicle can assist you with showing up at your fantasy objective or arriving at your next achievement regardless of what your objective might be.

Chapter 1

Objective Setting

Why Put fourth Objectives?
The absolute initial phase in your entire land plan is to make
an objective. It's hard to show up at an objective when you don't
understand what that objective is. How might you know whether you've
arrived at your variant of progress in the event that you don't initially characterize it?
Some of you may be asking why you can't simply attempt your best and see what occurs. The response is, obviously you could. In any case, I'm speculating you didn't get this book to
turn into a land financial backer of fair extent.
Regardless of whether you have big-shot measured dreams, you probably care about succeeding, and do as such as effectively as could really be expected. Without an objective, that most likely will not occur.
The world is brimming with interruptions. When you open your
eyes to the enterprising open doors accessible to you,
odds are very great that you'll see numerous thoughts that

look engaging. These new open doors can be categorized as one of

two classes: interruptions or space for development. It will be

essential to figure out how to separate between the two

furthermore, select unquestionably the most ideal choices (for you).

Sparkling article disorder is genuine! I have it. I dawned on me it very well may be amusing to stare off into space and miracle "imagine a scenario where" pursuing every single brilliant thought can dial you back. To

productively and actually arrive at your ideal objective,

you want to have a point of convergence to keep you on target and

pushing ahead. Exploring through each of the decisions life

tosses at you can be hard. Who would have no desire to open a

bistro, pimp out an RV, and travel cross-country as a

full-time vlogger, or at long last send off that new company

with your dearest companion? Those things sound like an

impact! Furthermore, they have very much potential for benefit. Why

not do every one of them? (That was a non-serious inquiry I will tell you

what difference would it make.) It tends to be not difficult to fall away from your most memorable expectations. Be that as it may

assuming you have a particular objective, you can spread out an arrangement that keeps you on the way to progress.

Tarl Yarber, a financial backer out of Seattle, once shared with me,

"You wouldn't recruit a worker for hire that had a fantasy of

building your home. You would enlist one who had an arrangement."

The ideal developer would have drawings, a gifted group of

workers, and a framework to carry out the culmination of your task. This is the means by which you ought to plan your objectives.

Your objective (your fantasy) necessities to have an arrangement set up.

You really want to ask yourself "What are the actionable steps that

will get me from where I'm to where I need to be?"

Begin with an objective and figure out it. Work

in reverse. Suppose that in something like five years, you need to procure

$5,000 in income a month. What number of units does that require? In the event that you can get $200 a month from a property in your market, you would have to acquire 25 properties (or units) to arrive at your objective.

Basically, you'd have to buy five properties each

year, for quite a long time. From that point, we can separate it from month to month, week by week, and also, everyday things to do. These things could go from calling banks to getting preapproved for a credit to

contacting three confidential moneylenders per week to dissecting

one arrangement daily. As we go through the book, you will fine-tune these things to do, yet for the time being, a decent spot to begin is to think about one undertaking you can do month to month, one errand you can do week after week, and one assignment you can do day to day.

For instance, one time per month, you could break down a new

market or neighborhood. One time per week, you could submit

a proposition, and one time each day, break down an arrangement. It sounds great in hypothesis, yet to get it going, you will need to allow

yourself things to do to finish and track these things.

Get things on paper. Set cutoff times and spread out unambiguous

directions. The more nitty-gritty you are in your arrangement, the

simpler it will be to execute it. This book is captioned "90 Days to Your

First Arrangement." Some of you will actually want to achieve the objectives in that measure of

time, however, nothing bad can be said about

picking an alternate course of events. You'll hear

I say it multiple times in this book, yet

do what works for you. Simply realize that it is

conceivable to get your most memorable arrangement in ninety

days .. assuming that you remain on track and propelled, what's more, above all, make a move!

Before we go excessively far, you want to achieve that very

initial step. You want to compose an objective.

Shut your eyes and picture your ideal objective.

What is it that you need to achieve in the following ninety days?

Is it to claim your most memorable speculation property? Is it to make

$15,000 off a house flip? Would you love to be a part of a group?

In all honesty, there is such an incredible concept as a terrible objective. I

try not to mean an objective that is untrustworthy or unlawful (in spite of the fact that

those unquestionably exist); an objective can terrible by be insufficient. In the event that you had a story plan and financial plan for a house you'd

like constructed, wouldn't that make it simpler than saying, "1

need a house"? By not determining your needs and needs, you are making it harder to control your result. Could

you envision attempting to construct a house when you can't really understand

what it ought to resemble? What materials would it be a good idea for you to utilize? What variety of beds would it be a good idea for you to pull from? Where might you indeed, even start? It would be a debacle, and furthermore profoundly improbable that the final product would be the one you want. The more focused your objective is, the better you will be

ready to make an arrangement and work out your things to do and,

accordingly, the more probable you will be to arrive at progress.

Outlining objective setting this way implies you could need to

run an organization that purchases multimillion-dollar business structures or you could need to live near the ocean and work

four hours every week. Both are choices: Everything relies upon your

vision, your way of life wishes, and your objectives.

Ordinarily, there are two various types of individuals.

Type #1: This sort of individual believes it's not difficult to distinguish

what they deeply desire, yet they battle to sort out

instructions to arrive.

Type #2: This sort of individual understands what they need to

do, yet not what they need. They can achieve undertakings, yet, they can't distinguish the ultimate objective or their ideal

objective.

Which kind of individual would you say you are? (Nor is awful, and you

may be a blend of both.) For instance, you might have

thought of what you need to acquire from putting resources into land.

what's more, know two or three significant stages to arrive. The

issue is that your arrangement is somewhat fluffy. It's not plainly

characterized and worked out. Or on the other hand, maybe you know the very way of life you need to live. You have everything impeccably planned,

directly down to the paint variety on the mass of your manor in the

mountains. In any case, you don't know which task on your rundown to tackle first. That is completely fine. As you flip through the pages of this book, you will be ready to adjust your objective and set up the pieces to

arrive. At the present time, you simply have to compose something

What do you need your land money management to help you

acquire? In the event that you are truly stuck for thoughts, ask a few companions or

relatives. Ideally, what might your life

seem to be? What might you invest your energy doing? What

sorts of things and encounters would you spend your

time and cash on? Record their responses. Record on paper your responses. Pose yourself with these inquiries before you go

to rest and allow your subliminal to concoct the

answers then you have your optimal way of life and objectives as a top priority, get them on paper. Post them where you can see them every day. The primary concern I trusted you've picked

up at this point is: MAKE An Objective

Examination loss of motion happens when you spend such an extended

time investigating and dissecting what is happening or the issue that

you keep yourself from making any genuine move. It very well may be

a major issue and occurs without your notification or assent,

so know! This objective setting step is essential, yet at the same, it's not permanently set up. Try not to harp on it so long that you stop

yourself from pushing ahead on your land process

furthermore, getting to the genuine work. You don't need to be a Genuine

Home Youngster for eternity!

I believe you should feel energized consistently to deal with your

things to do and to arrive at your objective. Your objective ought to

persuade you, it ought to drive you, and it ought to give you

perseverance. Recover profoundly and figure out what you need

out of life. Land gives you the chance to make

the way of life you need. Center around the way of life you want,

and afterward, we can assemble your land money management plan

around that.

Brilliant Objectives

Enough talking hypothetically. We should make some moves. You

may have known about Brilliant objectives. Brilliant Is an abbreviation

that is utilized to direct the advancement of quantifiable

objectives. A structure assists clients with distinguishing and

accomplishing great objectives. Your undertaking is to make an objective in which

every goal is:

• Quantifiable
• Reachable

• Important

• Time-arranged

For instance, prior I let you know that expressing, "l need to

own my most memorable investment property" is certainly not an extraordinary objective. In any case, it could

be. How about we apply the S.M.A.R.T. objective system? If rather you

said, "Through working in the land I need to make $250

of extra income every month so I can take care of my vehicle

advance before the year's over" that sounds Shrewd!

• Quantifiable: $250 income

• Reachable: dollar sum is absolutely feasible

• Important: through land

• Time-situated: before the year's over

When you have your Savvy objective, you can take it to the

next level with the extra abbreviation of MINS, in any case,

known as the Main Subsequent stage. What activity,

anyway little, could you at any point take to kick things off? What

could you at any point do after that to expand the distance or speed

your business ball will roll?

Go on, back away from this book. Do a little dreaming.

Dig deep. Imagine the daily routine you need to experience. What is

the load on your shoulders? Is it missing your child's

games? Not having the option to manage the cost of bills?

Can't uphold your guardians? What is it that you need and what is it that you need to

change in your life? Then, at that point, really record your objective. By writing these pieces down, you will acquire two
things: heading and inspiration. With these two powers driving your endeavors, beneficial things will occur!
Truly, feel free to record your objective on paper. I'll stand by. I
guarantee. A short time later, return and we'll continue on together. Alright? Great. You are above and beyond in the distance
furthermore, only a tad chomped to a lesser degree a youngster. However, we have quite a far to go. Objectives are perfect, yet all alone, they aren't sufficient. There are a couple of things you can do to capitalize on
your objective. Point of observation, I'm not saying you necessarily need to do these things. Everybody has their own tool compartment of methodologies that function admirably for them. At this moment, I need to propose not many that have worked for me and could work for you.
The Freshman's Tool compartment
Goal Diary
Actually, the meaning of "expectation" is like "objective"
however, I see it as the inclination behind an objective. The goal is
more about the feeling attached to the objective than the moves toward
accomplishing it. An aim is less unambiguous than an objective, yet
once drafted, it can uphold an individual's progress. "Expectations
assist with making greater lucidity and certainty around objectives and
associate us to the current second" says Liv Bowser,

the pioneer behind the psychological wellness organization Free.

An aim diary is a device you can use to record and

think about your objective-related goals. By finding an opportunity to

center around your goals, you are conveying to your

mind that this objective is significant. It merits your time and

worth your energy. What about some logical help? As indicated by

scholar Dr. Bruce Lipton, "The force of expectation has the capacity to change the state of our cerebrums in a real sense. This

process is known as brain adaptability the mind's delicate and

exchangeable potential, animated through the redundancy of

a specific way of behaving. With regard to goal setting,

brain connections are the path to self-advancing ways of behaving.

The more we rehash a positive goal or general positive

conduct, the more probable our cerebrum is to rearrange its neurons in support of ourselves. Through developing sound

goals, we are currently discovering that we have the capacity to

shape our minds in additional versatile and advantageous ways.""

Isn't excessively astonishing?

Recording your considerations about your goals can likewise

assist you with recognizing when your sentiments about your objectives shift, maybe flagging a leap forward or a longing to go in a

new bearing. Monitoring your own excursion on the

street to land achievement can assist you with celebrating scaled down

achievements, distinguish (and forestall future) negative

encounters turn continuously, and the sky is the limit from there.

test There is no incorrect way to an expectation diary. Profoundly

suggest looking at Brandon Turner's Goal

Diary found in the BiggerPockets book shop. You can write

down a bulleted rundown of goals, free-write in passage

style about your own appearance, or sketch out your

thoughts with pictures. Evaluate a couple of seasons of day and

techniques to find what turns out best for you. It very well may be

toward the start or end of the day. It could be every day,

midweek, or the final thing you do before you shut down for

the end of the week. This action could be a speedy five-minute

bulleted list or a strong half-hour of reflection. Making a

propensity that is charming and valuable is the reliable approach to

proceed with this propensity. Simply ensure this is certainly not a misuse of

time or something you are utilizing to put off really purchasing

land.

Time Impeding

Do you have any idea about where your time truly goes every day? Do

you at any point wind up arriving at the finish of a day (or week)

thinking, I felt occupied, however, what did I really achieve?" You're in good company. Assuming this is the kind of thing you battle

with, the data that comes next will be

supportive for you. Regardless of whether you figure you truly do use time well, you may be shocked by what you find when you do a

time study. We as a whole do things that sit around idly. Looking on friendly

media, gorging television, and rushing to the supermarket

on numerous occasions seven days as opposed to making one arranged trip are normal time killers. Shouldn't something is said about undertakings in our day that probably won't seem like time killers, yet are in fact

sucking up a colossal piece of our day, week, or month? What

on the off chance that you could be doing required errands in a manner that is more viable and proficient? These are incredible inquiries.

The most important phase in making a useful plan for getting work done is

taking a gander at how you utilize your time. The most ideal way is through

a period of study. As you travel as the day progressed, convey a

scratch pad or record a note in a telephone application. Each time you do an undertaking, change or switch a work area, compose it

• More spotlight on developing my portfolio to arrive at my objective,

perhaps need to hinder additional time on the schedule to check out

bargains. As well as recognizing time killers, a period study

assists certain individuals with understanding that they invest a ton of energy changing this way and that, either truly voyaging

starting with one spot then onto the next or intellectually exchanging between assignments.

In the event that you can figure out a way to opportunity block, doing related undertakings

during a particular and concentrated lump of your day or week, then you can eliminate pointless drive time

furthermore, weighty mental lifting. This will be incredibly useful.

Performing various tasks (or endeavoring to perform multiple tasks) utilizes oxygenated glucose, which fills your mind's capacity to zero in on an undertaking.

By zeroing in on significant undertakings in blocks of time rather

then plunging into them haphazardly throughout the day, you can

better utilize the physiological fuel assets that help you capability. At the point when you're intruded, it takes 23 minutes on normal to get once again into the zone.?

Simply consider all that time lost! Take a gander at your time to study

furthermore, perceive how you can all the more likely line up your undertakings and plan your day-to-day plan to stay away from this exorbitant error.

Responsibility Accomplice

Later on in the book, we will discuss building your group also, making organizations that cultivate achievement, yet there is

one individual you want to jump aboard immediately: a responsible accomplice. The best responsibility accomplice is

somebody who knows you and your objectives and will keep

you on target. Somebody who will check in with you and inquire

about your advancement. Somebody you trust. Somebody who spurs you. Somebody who comprehends the reason why the

highs are genuinely worth praising and why the lows are frustrating but on the other hand are illustrations educated. Somebody who

will assist you with bringing your dreams to reality.

Beginning your financial planning excursion can be desolate. Individuals

at present in your life may not grasp your new objectives; they might move you on your decision to put resources into a genuine

bequest. There will be high points and low points on the excursion, along

with many inquiries. Having a well-disposed individual in your

corner as you explore this excursion will make all the contrast.

I could converse with my folks about land until I'm blue in the face. While they'll continuously be strong for me and

my large dreams, they don't become as started up about market
examination and low loan fees as I do. Also, that is completely fine. Not
everybody must be energetic about exactly the same things. However,
That's what I trust if you have any desire to remain focused on an objective, you need to have somebody you can converse with who feels something similar. Luckily, there is a colossal organization of individuals on the web
(this is where I'm to conflict with each other's insight "of conversing with outsiders on the web") that you can interface with,
regardless of whether you have anybody in your family or companion circle
in the land game. BiggerPockets has over 2.5 million clients; there are many land financial planning Facebook gatherings, large numbers of which have a huge number of individuals. The people group is out there. One year, as an April Moron's Day trick, BiggerPockets declared they'd made an internet dating site for financial backers. I think most
individuals were vexed when they sorted out it wasn't correct!
Whether you interface with another financial backer on the web or at a
neighborhood meetup, there can be amazing open doors and advantages for both of you. One of the hardest characteristics to keep up with in
any undertaking is perseverance the perseverance to remain
roused as you break down a large number of arrangements, make offers, go over spending plans on recoveries, etc.

This is the junction at which you can relax on a responsibility accomplice the most, during the
battles, to ensure you don't surrender. A responsibility accomplice knows your objectives and activity plan. Their motivation is to keep you propelled and persistently dealing with your objective. This individual will uphold and
empower you, yet additionally, push you. Consequently, you will
respond and give something similar to them.
While picking a responsibility accomplice, consider the following:
• Try not to pick somebody whose main job is a team promoter.
• Ensure the individual makes them comprehends genuine domain contributing. Your responsibility association can be considerably more grounded assuming that the individual you pick has the same level (or higher) of land venture
information and encounters as you.
• Ensure both of you can set aside a few minutes
for responsibilities essential. There isn't anything more awful than
an uneven relationship.
• Remember that a responsibility accomplice doesn't
must be one individual. You can assemble a gathering. Once more, simply ensure everybody is committed.
Whenever you have tracked down your individual (or your kin), set
up a video call or an in-person meetup every month. When you initially begin, it could be useful to do several gatherings inside a brief time frame to get to know each other and focus on one another's objectives.

Keep in mind, this isn't a book club or companionship club. It's
a triumph bunch. You need to lead one another, regard
one another, and push one another. You need to hold each
other answerable for finishing things to do. Inspiring
each other as well as motivating. Assuming somebody is falling
behind and losing interest in their objective, then, at that point, it is your
obligation to tune in, endeavor to comprehend, and afterward
assist them with making an answer. There isn't anything better than
encircling yourself with similar people who are
hungry to succeed. Likewise, make it a point to toss a bit
of solid rivalry in with the general mish-mash. For some's
purposes, this can be incredibly persuading (and fun!).
Not certain how to find one of these astounding
responsibility accomplices? I take care of you. Take a stab at joining in
organizing occasions and nearby meetups.
My recommendation isn't simply to ask anybody out head long, "Do
you need to be my responsibility accomplice?" Get to be aware
of them first. Ensure they are the right fit and that you would be able
likewise to offer some benefit to them.
Your responsibility accomplice shouldn't just assist you
to keep focused yet, in addition, assist you with turning when required. Objective
setting is a consistent cycle that will be reset and

changed. Try not to be scared. Keep on track. Try not to beat

yourself up. Treat this as an excursion and comprehend you will

commit errors. Having a responsibility accomplice to pick you up when times are low will help.

Chapter 2

Land Effective financial planning Technique

As a land financial backer, you could experience changing guidance about effective money management on the web, virtual entertainment, and from different financial backers. A portion of these sources might guarantee they know best, yet there are numerous compelling systems for putting resources into land. There is certainly not a solitary technique that is the best methodology for each property manager. Truth be told, your land money management technique ought to mirror your own drawn-out objectives, accessible assets, and current conditions.

Furthermore, your financial planning technique can — and ought to — change as your requirements change. The progress of your rentals isn't attached to one contributing technique, but instead the abilities you've constructed, the strategies you've learned, and your capacity to move between various methodologies when required.

The following are six extraordinary land-effective money management systems you might use at different places in your effective financial planning profession:

1. House hacking

House hacking is a well-known financial planning methodology wherein you purchase a property, live fifty, and lease the other half out. The rental pay you get diminishes your month-to-month contract installments on the property.

This system functions admirably with duplexes and different multiplexes since you can keep an unmistakable division among your and your occupant's spaces. Be that as it may, a few financial backers likewise lease a cellar or room from their single-family home (SFH).

House hacking is an in-vogue and broadly involved financial planning technique in light of multiple factors. As far as one might be concerned, it's a brilliant method for changing to land-effective financial planning for new property managers. This is particularly obvious assuming you figure out how to deal with your leased unit or room with the property the executives are programming. Programming assists you with cautiously following your pay and costs while you lay out your business. One more advantage of house hacking is that it permits you to get a private home loan since you'll be residing on the property too.

Over the long haul, this procedure's point is to make it workable for you to move out and progress the property into an all-out rental.

2. BRRRR bargain

BRRRR contributing is another compelling methodology made well known by Brandon Turner on Greater Pockets. BRRRR represents purchase, recovery, lease, renegotiate, and rehash:

• Purchase: Purchase a property underneath market esteem.

• Recovery: Remodel and work on the property by adding esteem.

• Lease: Lease the property to cover the home loan.

•Renegotiate: Get the property reappraised, then use cash-out renegotiating to get a worthwhile home loan.

• Rehash: Utilize the capital you recuperated from the arrangement to put resources into additional properties.

With BRRRR, the thought is to exploit a property others might have ignored because of its low presumptive worth or clear absence of potential.

To utilize the BRRRR system, target properties that are sound ventures in spite of having serious room for improvement. Center around enhancements that increment esteem: introducing hardwood flooring, adding additional rooms, or renovating kitchens and restrooms. The worth added from these enhancements will further develop your property examination and assist you with tying down additional assets to contribute somewhere else.

3. Wholesaling/driving for dollars

Wholesaling is a procedure numerous financial backers use to benefit from extraordinary arrangements. In this system, you find a property that will make a fair setup, work with a deal between a purchaser and merchant, and afterward gather the contrast between the vendor's cost and the sum the purchaser pays.

To prevail with this technique, you should be educated about which properties are presently available. You can utilize famous posting locales, the Different Posting Administration (MLS), or a methodology known as "driving for dollars." This includes physically scanning neighborhoods for properties that look encouraging.

One disadvantage of wholesaling is that you really want solid promoting and deals abilities. On the off chance that you don't have this range of abilities and don't have any desire to attempt to secure it, wholesaling probably won't be for you.

4. Flipping properties

Flipping properties resemble BRRRR in that you purchase, remodel, and work on a property. Be that as it may, with house flipping, the ultimate objective is to sell the property, not lease it out.

House flipping works best when you revamp and flip as fast as could be expected. The more you hold on to sell, the more home loan installments you should make. Like BRRRR, house flipping works best with properties recorded at underneath market worth or those that are not difficult to improve at low expenses. Along these lines, upgrades can fundamentally build the property's estimation and lead to speedy turnovers.

One drawback to this methodology is that you'll have higher capital addition charges since you sold the property so rapidly. You'll likewise require help to effectively pull off house flipping — explicitly, you'll require a group of developers and renovators and admittance to great materials for a generally minimal price.

have higher capital addition charges since you sold the property so rapidly. You'll likewise require help to effectively pull off house flipping — explicitly, you'll require a group of developers and renovators and admittance to great materials for a somewhat minimal price.

5. Partnerships

A partnership is much of the time considered a more detached land money management system. Be that as it may, with cautious independent direction and a functioning eye on the cycle, a partnership can prompt incredible additions. The principal thought with the partnership technique is to pool your assets with other certified financial backers to purchase land.

This is the closely guarded secret: You pay partners to find and oversee most arrangements, then, at that point, benefit from the benefit. A partnership can be public or private. A public partnership is normally operationalized through a partnership commercial center, while a private partnership is overseen physically by financial backers.

Crowdfunding is a particular sort of partnership contributing that includes licensed and non-certify financial backers the same who contribute and benefit from bargains. In the event that you pick the crowdfunding way, you'll work with a more extensive scope of financial backers. You additionally will not be supposed to contribute as much section capital as you would with a conventional partnership (commonly just around $50-$1,000 is required).

In the event that you pick the partnership course, be finicky about who you work with. You need to guarantee your speculations are safe and sound, regardless of whether you contribute as much at first.

6. Live-in-then-lease

The live-in-then-lease system is a changed house-flipping situation. Basically, your property is an SFH (generally) that you live in at first and afterward transform into a rental after you move out. The fundamental distinction between live-in-then-lease and house hacking is that you don't reside in the property and lease it simultaneously. All things considered, these are two separate stages.

Live-in-then-lease is an extraordinary methodology for individuals who would rather not live intimately with their tenants yet at the same time need to take part in land financial planning on their spending plan.

With such countless ways of putting resources into land, it might appear to be trying to devise a system that addresses every one of your issues. In any case, by providing food with your financial planning methodology to your specific objectives, you can effectively develop your land business.

Chapter 3

Association

What is Association

An organization is a conventional game plan by at least two gatherings to oversee and work a business and offer its benefits.

Cash most times appear to be the major hindrance to engineers yet fortunately you don't need to bear the weight alone any longer. The association assists you with spreading the heaviness of the support and thereby expanding your rate achievement.

There are a few sorts of organizational plans. Specifically, in an organization business, all accomplices share liabilities and benefits similarly, while in others, accomplices might have restricted risk. There additionally is the alleged "quiet accomplice," in which one party isn't engaged with the everyday tasks of the business.

From a wide perspective, an organization can be any undertaking embraced together by numerous gatherings. The gatherings might be legislatures, not-for-profits ventures, organizations, or confidential people. The objectives of an organization likewise fluctuate broadly.

Inside the thin feeling of a for-benefit adventure embraced by at least two people, there are three primary classifications of organization: general organization, restricted association, and restricted obligation organization.

Sort of organization

General Association

In an overall organization, all gatherings share lawful and monetary responsibility similarly. The people are by and by liable for the obligations the association takes on. Benefits are additionally shared similarly. The particulars of benefit sharing will in all likelihood be spread out and recorded as a hard copy in an organization's understanding.

Restricted Responsibility Association

Restricted responsibility organizations (LLPs) are a typical design for experts, like bookkeepers, legal counselors, and engineers. This plan restricts accomplices' very own obligations so that, for instance, assuming one accomplice is sued for negligence, the resources of different accomplices are not in danger.

Restricted Association

Restricted organizations are half and half of general organizations and restricted responsibility associations. No less than one accomplice should be a general accomplice, with full private risk for the organization's obligations. Undoubtedly another is a quiet accomplice whose risk is restricted to the sum contributed. This quiet accomplice by and large doesn't take part in the administration or everyday activity of the partnership.

At long last, the clumsily named restricted obligation restricted organization is a new and somewhat remarkable assortment. This is a restricted organization that gives a more noteworthy safeguard from obligation for its general accomplices.

Benefits and Burdens of Organizations

A fruitful organization can assist a business with flourishing by permitting the accomplices to pool their work and assets. Most sole owners don't have the opportunity or assets to maintain an effective business alone, and the startup stage can be the most tedious.

Making an organization permits the accomplices to profit from each other's work, time, and skill. Besides, a wise accomplice can likewise give extra viewpoints and bits of knowledge that can assist the business with developing.

In any case, there is likewise an extra gamble in joining an organization. As well as sharing benefits, the accomplices may likewise take care of any misfortunes or obligations from different accomplices. There is likewise a higher opportunity of contention or fumble. At the point when the opportunity arrives to leave, agreeing about selling the business might be more enthusiastically.

Upsides and downsides of Organization

Experts

• Accomplices can pool their work, capital, and ability.

• Accomplices can share undertakings, permitting a more prominent balance between serious and fun activities.

• More accomplices can bring their experience

• More accomplices can carry their experience and new points of view to the firm.

Cons

• Accomplices might bring extra obligations or liabilities.

• There is a more noteworthy possibility of conflict or fumble.

• It might become more diligent to sell the business.

Chapter 4

Financing

What Is Financing

Financing is the method involved with giving assets to business exercises, making buys, or effective money management. Monetary establishments, like banks, are occupied with giving money to organizations, shoppers, and financial backers to assist them with accomplishing their objectives. The utilization of funding is imperative in any financial framework, as it permits organizations to buy items out of their nearby reach.

Put in an unexpected way, supporting is a method for utilizing the time worth of cash (TVM) to put future expected cash streams to use for projects that began today. Funding likewise exploits the way that a few people in an economy will have an overflow of cash that they wish to give something to do to produce returns, while others request cash to embrace venture (likewise with the desire for creating returns), making a business opportunity for cash.

Figuring out Financing

There are two principal sorts of support accessible for organizations: obligation funding and value funding. The obligation is a credit that should be repaid frequently with interest, yet it is ordinarily less expensive than raising capital due to burden derivation contemplations. Value needn't bother to be taken care of, yet it gives up possession stakes to the investor. Both obligation and value have their benefits and disadvantages.

Value Funding

"Value" is a different way to say proprietorship in an organization. For instance, the proprietor of a supermarket tie requirements to develop tasks. Rather than obligation, the proprietor might want to sell a 10% stake in the organization for $100,000, esteeming the firm at $1 million. Organizations like to sell value on the grounds that the financial backer bears all the gamble; assuming the business fizzles, the financial backer doesn't get anything.

Simultaneously, surrendering value is surrendering some control. Value financial backers need to have something to do with how the organization is worked, particularly in troublesome times, and are frequently qualified for votes in view of the number of offers held. In this way, in return for proprietorship, a financial backer gives cash to an organization and gets some case on future profit.

A few financial backers are content with development as offer cost appreciation; they maintain that the offer cost should go up. Different financial backers are searching for head assurance and pay-as-normal profits

Benefits of Value Supporting

Financing your business through financial backers enjoys a few benefits, including the accompanying:

• The greatest benefit is that you don't need to take care of the cash. Assuming that your business enters liquidation, your financial backer or financial backers are not lenders. They are part-proprietors in your organization, and therefore, their cash is lost alongside your organization.

• You don't need to make regularly scheduled installments, so there is much of the time more money available for working costs.

• Financial backers understand that it takes investment to fabricate a business. You will get the cash you really want without the tension of seeing your item or business flourishing in a short measure of time.

Disservices of Value Funding

Likewise, there are various detriments that accompany value funding, including the accompanying:

• What is your suggestion about having an alternative accomplice? At the junction when you put together value funding, it includes surrendering responsibility for part of your organization. The less secure the venture, the greater extent the stake the financial backer will need. You could need to surrender half or a greater amount of your organization, and except if you later develop an arrangement to purchase the financial backer's stake, that accomplice will take half of your benefits endlessly.

• You will also need to talk with your financial institution prior to deciding. Your organization is at this point not exclusively yours, and on the off chance that the financial backer has over half of your organization, you have a supervisor to whom you need to reply.

Obligation Supporting

A great many people know about obligation as a type of funding since they have vehicle credits or home loans. The obligation is likewise a typical type of funding for new organizations. Obligation funding should be reimbursed, and banks need to be paid a pace of revenue in return for the utilization of their cash.

A few moneylenders require security. For instance, expect the proprietor of the supermarket likewise concludes that they need another truck and should apply for a new line of credit for $40,000. The truck can act as security against the advance, and the supermarket proprietor consents to pay 8% interest to the moneylender until the credit is taken care of in five years.

The obligation is simpler to acquire for modest quantities of money required for explicit resources, particularly in the event that the resource can be utilized as a guarantee. While obligation should be repaid even in troublesome times, the organization holds possession and command over business tasks.

Benefits of Obligation Supporting

There are a few benefits to supporting your business through obligation:

• The loaning establishment has zero commands over how you run your organization, and it has no proprietorship.

• When you take care of the credit, your relationship with the loan specialist closes. That is particularly significant as your business turns out to be more important.

• The interest you pay on obligation supporting is charge deductible as a business expense.

• The regularly scheduled installment, as well as the breakdown of the installments, is a known cost that can be precisely remembered for your gauging models.

Burdens of Obligation Supporting

Obligation funding for your business comes with a few disadvantages:

• Adding an obligation installment to your month-to-month expenses expects that you will constantly have the capital inflow to meet all costs of doing business, including the obligation installment. For little or beginning phase organizations, that is frequently distant from certain.

• Independent company loaning can be eased back considerably during downturns. In harder times for the economy, it's more challenging to get obligation funding except if you are predominantly qualified.

Chapter 5

Structures your Group

The primary rule of group building is an undeniable one: to lead a group really, you should initially lay out your initiative with each colleague. Recollect that the best group pioneers fabricate their connections of trust and steadfastness, instead of dread or the force of their positions.

• Think about every worker's thoughts as important. Recall that a dumb thought can't really exist.

• Know about representatives' implicit sentiments. Set a guide to colleagues by opening up to representatives and being delicate to their temperaments and sentiments.

• Go about as a blending impact. Search for opportunities to intervene and determine minor debates; point persistently toward the group's more significant standards.

• Be clear while conveying. Be mindful so as to explain mandates.

• Energize trust and collaboration among representatives in your group. Recollect that the connections colleagues lay out among themselves are just as significant as those you lay out with them. As the group comes to fruition, give close consideration to the manners by which colleagues cooperate and do whatever it takes to further develop correspondence, participation, trust, and regard in those connections.

• Urge colleagues to share data. Underline the significance of each colleague's commitment and show how every one of their positions works together to draw the whole group nearer to its objective.

• Delegate critical thinking undertakings to the group. Allow the group to deal with intelligent fixes together.

• Work with correspondence. Recollect that correspondence is the absolute most significant figure of fruitful cooperation. Working with correspondence doesn't mean holding gatherings constantly. Rather it implies setting a model by staying open to ideas and worries, seeking clarification on some things and offering assistance, and giving your best to keep away from disarray in your own correspondence.

• Layout group values and objectives; assess group execution. Make certain to consult with individuals about the headway they are making toward laid out objectives so workers get a

sense both of their prosperity and of the difficulties that lie ahead. Address collaboration in execution principles. Talk about with your group:

• What do we truly think often about in playing out our work?

• How might the word achievement affect this group?

• What moves could we at any point initiate to satisfy our expressed qualities?

• Ensure that you have a reasonable thought of what you really want to achieve; that you understand what your guidelines for progress will be; that you have laid out clear time periods; and that colleagues figure out their obligations.

• Use agreement. Set targets, tackle issues, and plan for activity. While it takes significantly longer to lay out an agreement, this strategy eventually gives better choices and more prominent efficiency since it ties down each representative's obligation to all periods of the work.

• Set standard procedures for the group. These are the standards that you and the group layout to guarantee proficiency and achievement. They can be straightforward mandates (Colleagues are to be reliable for gatherings) or basic principles (Each colleague has the option to give suggestions and ideas), yet you ought to ensure that the group makes these standard procedures by agreement and focuses on them, both collectively and as people.

• Lay out a strategy for showing up at an agreement. You might need to lead an open discussion about the upsides and downsides of the proposition, or layout research advisory groups to explore issues and convey reports.

• Support tuning in and conceptualizing. As a boss, your primary goal in making an agreement is to animate the discussion. Recollect that workers are frequently hesitant to contradict each other and that this dread can lead your group to settle on unremarkable choices. At the point when you
empower banter you motivate inventiveness and that is the means by which you'll prod your group to improved results.

• Lay out the boundaries of agreement-building meetings. Be delicate to the dissatisfaction that can mount when the group isn't accomplishing agreement. At the start of your gathering, layout time cutoff points, and work with the group to accomplish agreement inside those boundaries. Keep an eye out for misleading agreements; in the event that an arrangement is struck excessively fast, be mindful so as to test individual colleagues to find their genuine sentiments about the proposed arrangement.

Chapter 6

Mechanization and programming

Does Your Realty Business Utilize Mechanization Programming?

Realtors are a bustling parcel and are truly taking care of numerous, confounded errands, here and there at the same time. From managing clients to overseeing promoting strategies (like online entertainment and lead age) and dealing with agreements and discussions, the obligations of real estate agents can overpower. This is where land robotization programming comes in.

Save Time, Cash, and Close More Leads!

In the realm of land, computerizing work processes and cycles is basic for some reasons; for example, mechanization programming saves you from doing dreary assignments like sending follow-up messages, which permits time to zero in on additional basic parts of your work - especially catching leads and sustaining prompts transform them into clients.

To be sure, there are numerous computerization apparatuses you can use to draw in and keep your leads and eventually help your land business. In any case, before we dig into that, see the reason why you really want to use the force of computerization programming:

Advantages of Mechanization Programming for Real estate agents

The top advantages of involving mechanization programming for your land business include:

• Deals pipe - Understanding the client venture - from where they show interest up to the place to checkout assists you with arranging the numerous phases of your client's commitment. You likewise get to see the regions you want to make acclimations to guarantee you are changing over additional individuals into clients.

• Lead division - Computerization programming incorporates highlights that permit you to isolate your clients into obvious gatherings for simpler administration. In that capacity, you can fabricate clients' profiles for a superior examination.

• Lead magnets - Lead magnets are fundamental for get-together additional information from planned clients. Robotization programming works with sending bulletins, preliminary memberships, tests, and so on, which contributes to catch more leads.

• Overseeing connections - Robotization programming can assist oversee outer associations with clients by further developing correspondence, giving customary criticism, tending to protests, and staying in contact with clients.

Top 10 Land Mechanization Programming Devices

Here are the main 10 mechanization devices that can be helpful for further developing your land business:

1. Parserr

One basic part of maintaining a land business is sending and getting messages, which frequently contain basic business information. Therefore, you really want programming that can help you concentrate and catch any significant lead information that comes through email (names, contact data, estimating, and so forth) so you can add it straightforwardly into your number one CRM, Google, or succeed sheet.

Parserr is a viable email parsing apparatus that can assist you with accomplishing this multitude of objectives: One of its remarkable benefits is it can coordinate with many other web-based applications. You can likewise involve it to separate information from reports and solicitations as well as request details, which permits you to have thorough information about your clients.

2. Spacio

Spacio is viable in computerizing the most common way of catching new leads at all your open houses, saving you the difficulty of gathering information physically. With this product, you can circle back to leads and even attach them to your number one CRM for support. You can likewise utilize gathered information to create reports that enticement for your clients' necessities and inclinations, which makes certain to build your possibilities of selling a house.

Spacio accompanies highlights like a custom enlistment structure for open house occasions (both face-to-face and virtual). You can likewise browse its three levels of bundles intended for specialists, groups, and organizations.

3. Dotloop

This extensive computerization programming is very helpful in the land business. It accompanies a few mechanized highlights, including instruments for virtual endorsement, text following and stockpiling, sharing, and structures, and that's only the tip of the iceberg. It additionally upholds a start-to-finish client experience where clients share significant issues and associations with different possibilities. With such a lot of effectiveness, you have a long list of motivations to coordinate Dotloop into your arrangement of instruments to assist with following your arrangements.

4. MeetEdgar

MeetEdgar is explicitly intended to help in your virtual entertainment-promoting endeavors. Basically, it computerizes your substance promoting, permitting you to share it to your online entertainment profiles, for example, Connected In, Facebook, Twitter, and Pinterest, with the snap of a button. Along these lines, you don't have to make content and post on numerous virtual entertainment channels, which saves you loads of opportunities to go to additional requesting assignments.

5. Specialist Legend

With Specialist Legend, you can undoubtedly mechanize customized messages, instant messages, and voice messages to smoothen the course of correspondence with clients. This product permits you to send customized phone messages, which is a certain approach to starting and supporting commitment with leads. Without Specialist Legend, you could find it trying to draw in hundreds or even a great many clients who need your administrations, which is clearly a detriment to your land business.

6. Open Home Pro

As well as robotizing the open house process, Open Home Master accompanies includes that show which leads merit circling back to so you can have the option to focus on the most encouraging clients. Besides, it offers fundamental CRM usefulness, for example, robotized merchant reports and lead the executives to assist you with breaking down the progress of your open houses. The product coordinates with web-based entertainment and email, making it conceivable to partake face to face and virtual house occasions with your crowd across various

7. Zurple

Zurple is #1 for realtors, because of its capacity to upgrade endeavors to follow and examine the way of behaving of leads. This product commonly gives computerized lead age that you can use to see which content is pertinent to each client in view of their pursuit history. With this data, you have thought of the leads you want to seek after and convert into clients.

8. Zillow Head Specialist

Throughout the long term, Zillow's Head Specialist has coordinated fundamental highlights that offer specialists ways of turning into the essential mark of concentration, which has altogether helped them support and close leads. Through the application, you can see the homes your leads are keen on, making it feasible for you to contact them with the

perfect message at the ideal time. It likewise accompanies a smoothed-out CRM with notes, versatile warnings, and updates.

9. Autopilot

Another high-priority land robotization programming is Autopilot. As one of the most far-reaching programming, it offers a few mechanization instruments, including CRM incorporation, client venture maps, client conduct following, and examination. You will likewise approach highlights

like leading the board, multichannel promoting, and leading the executives. With Autopilot, you make certain to make some simple memories envisioning your advanced advertising endeavors.

10. ReboGateway

ReboGateway is the right device for taking care of the vast majority of the backend processes, explicitly those that worry about monetary exchanges: As a specialist, you are engaged with various cash bargains that you really want to ensure are a sans mistake. On account of ReboGateway, you have the ideal apparatus for coordinating your exchanges, which ensures safe monetary arrangements.

CONCLUSION

Come-by results as is notable take consistency and time. You don't fire up a business today and expect returns right away, it requires investment. It could seem as though others went through a similar cycle with a more limited time span however yours is taking more time, and that isn't reason enough for you to stop. You need to endlessly push till your ideal outcome is conveyed right to your hands. The land is the new mother lode and mining gold doesn't come simple yet the profits are generally worth the work. Remain through to your interest.

www.ingramcontent.com/pod-product-compliance
Lightning Source LLC
Chambersburg PA
CBHW071144220526
45467CB00015B/1917